Figurative Langua

and Other Literary Devices

For Grades 3–6

Written by Rebecca Stark
Illustrated by Karen Birchak
Educational Books 'n' Bingo

ISBN-13: 978-1-56644-531-3

Printed in the U.S.A.

TABLE OF CONTENTS

TO THE TEACHER

Literary techniques are the constructions of language used by an author to convey meaning. These techniques make the story more interesting to the reader. It is crucial that students learn to identify and understand these constructions. Familiarity with these techniques will prepare them not only for standardized tests, but also for their future education. The understanding of these devices will help students get more enjoyment from the fiction they read—both in and out of the classroom situation. This comprehensive unit uses examples from classic and modern literature to introduce and reinforce these techniques.

LITERARY DEVICES

The following literary terms / techniques are covered in this text:

- Connotation
- Dialogue
- Dialect
- Imagery
- Idiom
- Simile
- Metaphor
- Allusion
- Personification
- Anthropomorphism
- Hyperbole
- Understatement
- Oxymoron
- Symbol
- Pun
- Alliteration
- Onomatopoeia

FORMAT

Each term is defined. One or more examples are given from classic and/or modern literature. Students are then given opportunities to identify, explain, and use the technique.

Figurative Language & Other Literary Devices for Grades 3–6 is designed to teach students literary terms and techniques to help them understand and analyze works of fiction.

At the end of this unit, students will be able to …
- identify the style of a work of literature;
- understand denotation and connotation;
- identify and understand dialogue;
- identify and understand dialect;
- identify and understand imagery;
- identify and understand idioms, adages, and proverbs;
- identify and understand similes and metaphors;
- identify and understand allusion;
- identify and understand personification;
- identify and understand anthropomorphism;
- identify and understand hyperbole;
- identify and understand understatement;
- identify and understand oxymora;
- identify and understand symbolism;
- identify and understand puns and other plays on words;
- identify and understand onomatopoeia and alliteration;
- use all of the above to help them analyze works of literature; and
- use figurative language and other literary techniques in their own writing.

Common Core State Standards

The activities in this book will help you implement these Common Core State Standards:

Anchor Standards

CCSS.ELA-Literacy.CCRA.R.4 – Interpret words and phrases as they are used in a text, including determining technical, connotative, and figurative meanings, and analyze how specific word choices shape meaning or tone.

CCSS.ELA-Literacy.CCRA.L.5 - Demonstrate understanding of figurative language, word relationships, and nuances in word meanings.

ELA Standards: Literature

CCSS.ELA-Literacy.RL.3.4 – Determine the meaning of words and phrases as they are used in a text, distinguishing literal from nonliteral language.

CCSS.ELA-Literacy.RL.4.4 – Determine the meaning of words and phrases as they are used in a text, including those that allude to significant characters found in mythology (e.g., Herculean).

CCSS.ELA-Literacy.RL.5.4 – Determine the meaning of words and phrases as they are used in a text, including figurative language such as metaphors and similes.

CCSS.ELA-Literacy.RL.6.4 – Determine the meaning of words and phrases as they are used in a text, including figurative and connotative meanings; analyze the impact of a specific word choice on meaning and tone.

ELA Standards: Language

CCSS.ELA-Literacy.L.3.5 - Demonstrate understanding of figurative language, word relationships and nuances in word meanings.

CCSS.ELA-Literacy.L.4.5a - Explain the meaning of simple similes and metaphors (e.g., as pretty as a picture) in context.

CCSS.ELA-Literacy.L.4.5b - Recognize and explain the meaning of common idioms, adages, and proverbs.

CCSS.ELA-Literacy.L.5.5a - Interpret figurative language, including similes and metaphors, in context.

CCSS.ELA-Literacy.L.5.5b - Recognize and explain the meaning of common idioms, adages, and proverbs.

CCSS.ELA-Literacy.L.6.5a - Interpret figures of speech (e.g., personification) in context.

Literary Devices

Literary Devices of Style

An author's **style** is the way he or she uses language. It can be formal or informal. One of the most important factors is **word choice.** Some authors use vocabulary that is simple and direct; others choose to use more elaborate or unusual vocabulary. Many words with similar denotations, or dictionary meanings, have different connotations. In other words, they evoke different feelings and thoughts. Lastly, the use of idioms, dialogue, and dialect are other ways in which word choice can influence a writer's style; all of these things tend to make the style more informal.

The use of **literary techniques** also affects the style. A common technique is imagery. Imagery appeals to the reader's senses—sight, sound, smell, touch, and taste. These images help the reader form a mental picture of what is happening in the story.

Many authors use some form of **figurative language**. The term "figurative" means that the words are not meant to be taken literally. Figurative language encourages readers to use their imagination and to look at the world in new ways. Among the most common forms of figurative language are simile, metaphor, and personification. Other forms include pun, hyperbole, understatement, and oxymoron. Authors also use **poetic devices** that rely on sound; alliteration and onomatopoeia are examples.

Common Literary Devices

The following literary devices of style are explained in this worktext:

- Connotation
- Dialogue
- Dialect
- Imagery
- Idiom
- Simile
- Metaphor
- Allusion
- Personification
- Anthropomorphism
- Hyperbole
- Understatement
- Oxymoron
- Symbolism
- Pun
- Alliteration
- Onomatopoeia

Connotation

It is important to understand denotation and connotation when reading a work of literature. **Denotation** is the clearly expressed meaning of a word or phrase. In other words, it is the dictionary definition. **Connotation** is the associated meaning of a word or phrase. For example, the words *slender* and *skinny* have similar denotations: "having little width in proportion to the height or length." However, they have different connotations. Think about the following two sentences:

> Rebecca is a skinny girl with brown hair.
>
> Rebecca is a slender girl with brown hair.

The first sentence makes us think that Rebecca is too thin. The second makes us think that she is gracefully thin.

EXAMPLE FROM LITERATURE

From Because of Winn Dixie, by Kate DiCamillo
Opal has given her father a lozenge to taste.
Upon tasting it he says, "It has a peculiar flavor."

Does the word *peculiar* make you think that the lozenge has a good taste or a bad taste?

Opal went on to explain that the lozenge tastes bad because the inventor had just lost his entire family.

What if he had described the flavor as *unusual* or *out of the ordinary?* All three—*peculiar, unusual,* and *out of the ordinary*—mean "uncommon," but each has a different connotation.

How would the use of these terms have changed your inference about the taste?

_____

_____

_____

_____

_____

_____

_____

_____

_____

Negative Connotations

For each set, circle the word that has the most negative connotation. Be aware that what has a favorable connotation for you may have an unfavorable one for someone else and vice versa! Be prepared to explain your choice if it differs from the given answer.

1. house
   cottage
   mansion
   shack

2. slender
   thin
   trim
   scrawny

3. assignment
   chore
   mission
   task

4. ask
   interrogate
   request
   question

5. aroma
   odor
   scent
   stench

6. walk
   stroll
   meander
   trudge

7. frugal
   economical
   thrifty
   cheap

8. unique
   outlandish
   exceptional
   unusual

9. talk
   speak
   babble
   converse

10. copy
    mock
    mimic
    imitate

11. curious
    inquisitive
    interested
    snoopy

12. reserved
    quiet
    withdrawn
    shy

Dialogue

Dialogue is a conversation between two or more characters. It can do a lot to arouse our interest and spark our curiosity! Dialogue is often used by an author to bring the story to life. Because people usually speak in a more informal manner than the way in which they write, dialogue tends to make the style more informal.

Dialogue can add to a story in several ways. Sometimes it helps the reader determine the setting of a story. It can inform the reader about an event that has occurred in the past. It can also help the reader predict an event that may occur in the future. Often we learn a lot about the characters from the words they speak and from the way others speak to them.

EXAMPLES FROM LITERATURE

From *Heidi,* by Johanna Spyri

The following dialogue is between Heidi's Aunt Detie and a woman named Barbie.

" 'I'm taking her up to Uncle. She'll have to stay with him now.'

'What, stay with Uncle Alp on the mountain? You must be crazy. How can you think of such a thing? But of course he'll soon send you about your business if you suggest that to him.'

'Why should he? He's her grandfather and it's high time he did something for her.' "

The author used dialogue to tell the readers that Heidi is being taken by her Aunt Detie to live with her grandfather and that Barbie does not think it is a good idea. We also learn something about the setting: the grandfather lives on the mountain. Although we cannot be sure from this excerpt, we might also infer that Detie has been caring for Heidi until now and no longer wants to do so.

From *Lily's Crossing,* by Patricia Reilly Giff

This dialogue is a conversation between Lily and her friend Margaret.

Lily says to Margaret, " 'Poppy's not going overseas. ... He's an engineer. He's important right where he is.' "

Margaret responds, " 'My father says he [Lily's father] probably would go this summer.' "

Lily then exclaims, " 'Your father's wrong!' "

The dialogue helps us know that there is a war going on. We can predict from the conversation that Lily's father will likely be sent overseas.

Uses of Dialogue

Dialog can serve many purposes.

- It may help develop the setting.

- It may explain an event that has already occurred.

- It may predict an event that may (or may not) occur.

- It may provide insight into one or more characters.

- It may be used to arouse interest.

- It may be used to create suspense.

What's the Purpose?

Read each example and think about the purpose or purposes the dialogue serves.

1. The following dialogue is from *Heidi*. It is a continuation of the conversation between Detie and Barbie. What does the dialogue tell us about the grandfather and about the setting?

" 'Well, I'm glad I'm not that poor child. ... Nobody really knows what's the matter with that old man, but he won't have anything to do with anybody, and he hasn't set foot in a church for years. When he does come down from the mountain ... everybody scuttles out of his way.' "

_____

_____

_____

_____

_____

2. The following are excerpts from *The Witch of Blackbird Pond,* by Elizabeth George Speare. What purpose does this dialogue serve?

Nat says to Kit, " 'There's Connecticut Colony. You've come a long way to see it.' "

Kit asks, " 'Is that Wethersfield?' "

Nat explains, " 'Oh, no, Wethersfield is some way up the river. This is the port of Saybrook.' "

The captain's wife says to Kit, " 'Aye, didn't I tell you I'd be leaving you at Saybrook? But don't look so sad, child. 'Tis not far to Wethersfield, and we'll be meeting again.' "

_____

_____

_____

_____

_____

_____

Charlotte's Web

Charlotte's Web, by E.B. White, is filled with dialogue. The following is a conversation between Fern and her father.

Fern Arable: "But it's unfair. The pig couldn't help being born small, could it? If I had been very small at birth, would you have killed me?"

Mr. Arable: "Certainly not. But this is different. A little girl is one thing, a runty pig is another."

Fern Arable: "I see no difference. This is the most terrible case of injustice I ever heard of."

Mr. Arable: "All right. You go back to the house and I will bring the runt when I come in. I'll let you start it on a bottle, like a baby. Then you'll see what trouble a pig can be."

1. What do we learn about the setting of the story?

_____

_____

2. What do we learn about Fern?

_____

_____

_____

_____

3. What do we learn about Mr. Arable?

_____

_____

_____

_____

4. In your opinion, why did Mr. Arable change his mind?

_____

_____

_____

_____

Creating Dialogue

Choose one of the following situations. Create a dialogue that might be used in a story based upon that situation. Your dialogue should provide relevant information about the plot, one or more of the characters, the setting, or another aspect of the story.

SITUATION

You just won two tickets to a concert, game, or other special event. You have two best friends, but can only invite one of them.

DIALOGUE #1

Between you and the friend you are inviting.

_____ : _____

_____

_____ : _____

_____

_____ : _____

_____

_____ : _____

_____

DIALOGUE #2

Between you and the friend you are not inviting.

_____ : _____

_____

_____ : _____

_____

_____ : _____

_____

_____ : _____

_____

Dialect

Sometimes an author uses dialect when creating dialogue. **Dialect** is speech that reflects the vocabulary, speech patterns, and grammar of a particular geographic region or of a particular social or economic group. The use of dialect can help create the tone of the book. The tone can be serious or lighthearted; it can be objective or it can reflect the author's point of view; it can be conversational or formal; and so on.

EXAMPLES FROM LITERATURE
From *Shiloh,* by Phyllis Reynolds Naylor

Grammar
The author uses unconventional contractions and improper grammar to create realistic dialogue often encountered in the hills of West Virginia, where the story is set.

Unconventional Contraction: ***better'n*** for *better than*
Improper Grammar: Funny how he **don't** make a sound.
Leaving out the Word *I*: **Heard** somebody say...

Vocabulary
The author uses vocabulary and idiomatic expressions often used in the hills of West Virginia.

"I want you to **quit** going on about it."
"Looks like he's **fixing to** follow me all the way to our house."
"Don't know what else **I figured** Dad to say."
"Around here folks **keep to their own business.**"

Speech Patterns
The speakers often leave off the final "g": ***yellin', tellin', sittin', mornin', doin',*** and so on.

The speakers often leave off the beginning letter(s): ***'em*** for *them,* ***'cept*** for *except,* ***'bout*** for *about,* and so on.

Interpreting Dialect

These excerpts from well-known works of literature contain dialect. Rewrite them replacing the phrases in bold with standard English.

1. From *Shiloh,* by Phyllis Reynolds Naylor
The author uses expressions often used in the hills of West Virginia, where the story is set.
Situation: Ray Preston and Marty have gone to ask Judd Travers if Shiloh is his dog. Marty, as the narrator, explains the following:

"**Up here in the hills** you hardly ever **get down to business right off.** First you **say your howdys** and then you talk about anything else **but what you come for. …**"

_____

_____

_____

_____

2. From *Shiloh,* by Phyllis Reynolds Naylor
Situation: Marty's dad is a mail carrier. People have been leaving food for him in their mailboxes and he doesn't know why.

" 'Folks are **taking to leavin'** me food in their mailboxes, Lou. **Used to be** it was just Mrs. Ellison and her banana bread, but **found me** a ham sandwich today.' "

_____

_____

_____

_____

3. From *Bud, Not Buddy,* by Christopher Paul Curtis
Situation: Bud does not understand much of what the men in the band say to him.

In Chapter 16, Steady Eddie says to Bud, " '**Cop a squat.**' "
Bud figured out what Eddie meant because Steady Eddy pointed to a chair.

Use your inferencing skills to determine what Steady Eddie meant.

_____

_____

What Is Imagery?

Authors use **imagery** to create mental pictures by appealing to their readers' senses: sight, sound, touch, smell, and taste. Imagery can add to a work of fiction in several ways. It may help the author create a particular mood and cause readers to feel certain emotions. Sometimes imagery helps readers learn more about the characters. Imagery can also be used to develop a theme.

TYPES OF IMAGES:

SIGHT
Visual images refer to things we can see. They appeal to our sense of sight.

SOUND
Auditory images refer to things we can hear. They appeal to our sense of sound.

TOUCH
Tactile images refer to things we can feel. They appeal to our sense of touch.

SMELL
Olfactory images refer to things we can smell. They appeal to our sense of smell.

TASTE
Gustatory images refer to things we can taste. They appeal to our sense of taste.

Also ...

ACTIONS
Kinesthetic images refer to actions or motions. They, too, help create a mental picture of what is happening.

Imagery

EXAMPLE FROM LITERATURE:
From *Out of the Dust,* by Karen Hesse

The Great Plains area of the United States suffered a severe drought during the 1930s. The region became known as The Dust Bowl. In *Out of the Dust,* Karen Hesse describes what life was like for the people living through the disaster. She tells the story in the form of poems written by a fourteen-year-old girl in her journal. The poems are filled with imagery.

Unlike the imagery in most of the book's poems, the imagery in this poem creates an optimistic mood.

Apples (June 1934)

Ma's **apple blossoms**
have turned to **hard green balls.**

To eat them now,
so **tart,**
would turn my mouth inside out,
would make my **stomach groan.**

But in just a couple months,
after the baby is born,
those apples will be ready
and we'll make **pies**
and **sauce**
and **puddings**
and **dumplings**
and **cake**
and **cobbler**

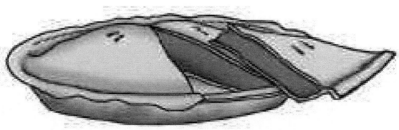

and have just plain **apples** to take to school
and **slice** with my pocket knife
and **eat** one **juicy piece** at a time
until my **mouth is clean**
and fresh
and my **breath is nothing but apple.**

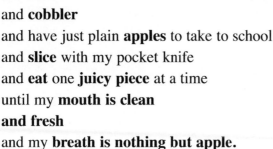

Imagery in *The Wind in the Willows*

Kenneth Grahame made excellent use of imagery in his novel *The Wind in the Willows*. Think about the mental pictures created by the phrases in bold. Then fill in the chart on the following page.

1. From Chapter I: The River Bank

"The Mole had been working very hard all the morning, spring-cleaning his little home. First with brooms, then with dusters; then on ladders and steps and chairs, with a brush and a pail of whitewash; till he had **dust in his throat and eyes**, and **splashes of whitewash** all over his **black fur,** and an **aching back** and **weary arms.** Spring was moving in the air above and in the earth below and around him, penetrating even his dark and lowly little house with its spirit of divine discontent and longing. ... So he scraped and scratched and scrabbled and scrooged and then he **scrooged** again and **scrabbled** and **scratched** and **scraped, working busily** with his **little paws** and **muttering** to himself, 'Up we go! Up we go!' till at last, **pop!** his snout came out into the **sunlight**, and he found himself **rolling** in the **warm grass** of a **great meadow.**

'This is fine!' he said to himself. 'This is better than whitewashing!' The **sunshine** struck **hot on his fur**, **soft breezes caressed his heated brow**, and after the seclusion of the cellarage he had lived in so long the **carol of happy birds** fell on his dulled hearing almost like **a shout**. **Jumping off** all his four legs at once, in the joy of living and the delight of spring without its cleaning, he pursued his way across the meadow till he reached the hedge on the further side."

2. From Chapter IV: Mr. Badger

The floor was **well-worn red brick**, and on the wide hearth burnt a **fire of logs**, between two attractive chimney-corners tucked away in the wall, well out of any suspicion of draught [draft]. A couple of high-backed settles, facing each other on either side of the fire, gave further sitting accommodations for the sociably disposed. ... Rows of spotless plates winked from the shelves of the dresser at the far end of the room, and from the rafters overhead hung **hams,** bundles of **dried herbs, nets of onions,** and **baskets of eggs. ...**

The kindly Badger **thrust** them down on a settle to **toast themselves at the fire**, and bade them remove their **wet coats** and boots. Then he fetched them dressing-gowns and slippers, and himself bathed the Mole's shin with **warm water** and mended the cut with sticking-plaster till the whole thing was just as good as new, if not better. In the embracing **light and warmth**, **warm and dry** at last, with **weary legs** propped up in front of them, and a suggestive **clink of plates** being arranged on the table behind, it seemed to the storm-driven animals, now in safe anchorage, that the **cold** and trackless Wild Wood just left outside was miles and miles away, and all that they had suffered in it a half-forgotten dream."

Chart the Images

For each bold word or phrase on the previous two pages, think about the sense or senses to which the author is appealing. Then fill in the chart. You may place an image in more than one category.

APPEAL TO SENSE OF SIGHT

APPEAL TO SENSE OF SOUND

APPEAL TO SENSE OF TOUCH

APPEAL TO SENSE OF SMELL OR TASTE

REFER TO ACTIONS

Create a Mental Picture

Choose one of the following experiences and write a descriptive paragraph about it. Use as many different types of images as you can.

A Day at the Circus

A Day at the Beach

A Trip to the Zoo

In a Bakery

At an Ice-Cream Parlor

In an Airport

_____

_____

_____

_____

_____

_____

_____

_____

_____

_____

_____

_____

_____

_____

_____

_____

_____

Figurative Language

Figurative language is the use of language in a way that differs from the original, intended meaning of the word or words. In other words, the words should not be taken literally. Sometimes we refer to the various forms of figurative language as "figures of speech."

FORMS OF FIGURATIVE LANGUAGE

Idiom

Simile

Allusion

Metaphor

Personification

Hyperbole

Understatement

Oxymoron

Symbol

Pun

Idioms

An **idiom** is a figure of speech that does not make sense if you take each individual element literally. For example, suppose someone said, "It's raining cats and dogs." Most people would understand that it is raining heavily; they would not expect to see animals falling from the sky!

Some idioms, like the one above, become so common that they lose their effectiveness; we call overused figures of speech **clichés**. It's best not to use clichés too often in your writing, especially if you can think of a more original way to express your idea.

EXAMPLES FROM LITERATURE

From *A Year Down Yonder,* by Richard Peck

Situation: Mary Alice has been sneaking treats from her plate to feed the cat.

"Grandma knew. She **had eyes in the back of her head.**"

"To have eyes in the back of one's head" is an idiom. It means that the person seems to be able to sense what is going on outside his or her field of vision.

From *Maniac Magee,* by Jerry Spinelli

Situation: Maniac Magee surprises people he doesn't know by greeting them.

"They stopped. They … wondered: Do I know that kid? Because people just didn't say that to strangers, **out of the blue.**"

"Out of the blue" is an idiom. It means that something has happened unexpectedly. We cannot take the words literally.

Working with Idioms

For each excerpt, replace the portion in bold with standard English.

1. From *The Wind in the Willows,* by Kenneth Grahame
Situation: Mole was sitting on the grass, looking across the river.

"As he sat on the grass and looked across the river, a dark hole in the bank opposite, just above the water's edge, **caught his eye,** and dreamily he fell to considering what a nice snug dwelling-place it would make ..."

_____

_____

_____

2. From *Dear Mr. Henshaw,* by Beverly Cleary

Situation: Leigh's parents have divorced and his father never calls when he says he will.

"I sure wish Dad lived with us again, but he said he would phone in about a week and **to keep my nose clean."**

_____

_____

_____

3. From *Bud, Not Buddy,* by Christopher Paul Curtis

Situation: Steady Eddy, a saxophonist, has asked Bud to put the case with his saxophone in the car.

" 'And be careful, that's my **bread and butter** in there. ' "

_____

_____

_____

Some Common Idioms

to cross that bridge

to be one's bread and butter

to let the cat out of the bag

to put one's foot down

to catch one's eye

out of the blue

to be at the end of one's rope

to pull one's leg

to be tongue tied

to cook up a storm

to lend a hand

to put on one's face

to draw the line

to be on thin ice

to pull strings

to bury the hatchet

to be all thumbs

to keep one's nose clean

to have cold feet

to have a green thumb

to be a dime a dozen

to bite one's tongue

a wolf in sheep's clothing

to be easy as pie

to burn one's bridges

icing on the cake

to turn over a new leaf

to have a chip on one's shoulder

to hold one's tongue

a taste of one's own medicine

to be in the same boat

to lose one's head

to be a chip off the old block

to lend an ear

to bite the hand that feeds one

to be a third wheel

to be on the same page

to be on the house

to keep an eye on someone

to rock the boat

Add five common idioms to the list.

_____

_____

_____

_____

_____

Guess the Idiom

Try to figure out the missing idiom. Choose from the list on the previous page. Change pronouns, verb forms, etcetera, as necessary.

1. From *Because of Winn Dixie,* by Kate DiCamillo

Situation: Opal has just told Gloria Dump about missing her mother. Gloria suggests that Opal may have gotten more from her mother than her looks and her ability to run fast.

Gloria says, " 'Could be that you got more of your mama in you than just red hair and freckles and running fast … Like maybe you got her _____.
The two of us could plant something and see how it grows.' "

2. From *A Year Down Yonder,* by Richard Peck

Situation: Mary Alice has been followed home by a bully who is trying to get a dollar from her. Mary Alice is frustrated and does not know what to do.

"I guess I was glad to see Grandma there on the porch. I don't know. I was pretty much

_____."

3. From *Tales of a Fourth Grade Nothing,* by Judy Blume

Situation: Overnight guests were expected, and Mom was preparing for their arrival.

"She spent the day in the kitchen _____."
She used so many pots and pans Fudge didn't have any left to bang together."

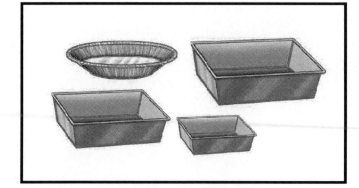

Guess the Idiom, Continued

4. From *Treasure Island,* by Robert Louis Stevenson

Situation: Dr. Livesey is afraid that the squire will talk of their plan to seek the treasure.

Dr. Livesey: "There's only one man I'm afraid of."
The squire: "And who's that?"
Dr. Livesey: "You, for you cannot _____."

5. From *Tales of a Fourth Grade Nothing,* by Judy Blume

Situation: Peter as narrator is talking about Dr. Brown, the family dentist. Dr. Brown is also a good friend of Peter's father.

"They went to school together. He's always saying he takes special care of me and Fudge because we're _____."

6. From *Tales of a Fourth Grade Nothing,* by Judy Blume

Situation: Peter is describing his father's secretary.

"She has the longest eyelashes I've ever seen. Once I heard my mother say, 'Janet must have to get up at the crack of dawn to _____.' "

7. From *James and the Giant Peach,* by Roald Dahl

Situation: James has crawled inside a giant magic peach and meets Ladybug, Grasshopper, Centipede, and other oversized creatures. He is very frightened.

" 'You mustn't be frightened,' the Ladybug said kindly. 'We wouldn't *dream* of hurting you. You are one of us now, didn't you know that? You are one of the crew. We're _____ _____.' "

Adages and Proverbs

Adages and proverbs are wise sayings. An adage is a traditional saying that many people accept as the truth. It is defined in the *Merriam-Webster Dictionary* as "an old and well-known saying that expresses a general truth; a saying often in metaphorical form that embodies a common observation." A proverb is a short, popular saying that also seems to hold some truth. It is defined in the *Merriam-Webster Dictionary* as "a brief popular saying that gives advice about how people should live or that expresses a belief that is generally thought to be true." Many use the terms *adage* and *proverb* interchangeably.

Adage: Good things come in small packages.
Proverb: There's no use crying over spilt milk.

EXAMPLES FROM LITERATURE

From *Anne of Green Gables,* by L. M. Montgomery
Situation: Anne is upset because she thinks she is homely. Marilla has told her not to be vain.

" 'How can I be vain when I know I am homely?' " protested Anne. . . .

" 'Handsome is as handsome does,' " quoted Marilla.

Aesop's Fables
Aesop lived from about 620–564 BCE. He is credited with writing many fables, each of which had a moral, or lesson, at the end. Many of these morals have become well-known proverbs and adages.

The Fox and the Goat

A Fox one day fell into a deep well and could find no means of escape. A Goat, overcome with thirst, came to the same well, and seeing the Fox, inquired if the water was good. Concealing his sad plight under a merry guise, the Fox indulged in a lavish praise of the water, saying it was excellent beyond measure, and encouraging him to descend. The Goat, mindful only of his thirst, thoughtlessly jumped down, but just as he drank, the Fox informed him of the difficulty they were both in and suggested a scheme for their common escape. "If," said he, "you will place your forefeet upon the wall and bend your head, I will run up your back and escape, and will help you out afterwards." The Goat readily agreed and the Fox leaped upon his back. Steadying himself with the Goat's horns, he safely reached the mouth of the well and made off as fast as he could. When the Goat reproached him for breaking his promise, he turned around and cried out, "You foolish old fellow! If you had as many brains in your head as you have hairs in your beard, you would never have gone down before you had inspected the way up, nor have exposed yourself to dangers from which you had no means of escape."

Look before you leap.

Good Advice!

Part 1: Add two adages or proverbs to the list below.

ADAGES and PROVERBS

Where there's smoke, there's fire.

Actions speak louder than words.

You win some, you lose some.

Two wrongs don't make a right.

Don't judge a book by its cover.

Don't cut off your nose to spite your face.

A watched pot never boils.

Opposites attract.

Look before you leap.

You can't teach an old dog new tricks.

Practice makes perfect.

Stop and smell the roses.

Haste makes waste.

A penny saved is a penny earned.

_____   _____

Part 2: Choose three sayings from the list above. Use each in a brief dialogue.

Example: This is a conversation between Jane and her mother.

Jane: I completed my homework in record time, but Mrs. Jonas said I made many mistakes.

Mother: Haste makes waste!

1. This is a conversation between _____ and _____.

_____: _____

_____

_____: _____

_____

2. This is a conversation between _____ and _____.

_____: _____

_____

_____: _____

_____

3. This is a conversation between _____ and _____.

_____: _____

_____

_____: _____

_____

Metaphors and Similes

Both metaphors and similes are figures of speech that compare two unlike things. A **simile** makes the comparison clearly, usually by using the words *like* or *as*. A **metaphor** does not use *like* or *as* to make the comparison. In other words, a simile says something is *like* something else. A metaphor says something *is* something else.

EXAMPLES FROM LITERATURE
From *James and the Giant Peach,* by Roald Dahl

Roald Dahl used many similes and metaphors in his novel *James and the Giant Peach.*

SIMILES
In Chapter 1 the woods, fields and ocean, all of which James could see from the garden, are described. They are compared to a magic carpet.

"He used to spend hours every day standing at the bottom of the garden, gazing wistfully at the lovely but forbidden world of **woods and fields and ocean that spread below him like a magic carpet.**"

This excerpt from Chapter 5 compares Aunt Sponge, who is extremely short and fat, to a jelly-fish.

"Aunt Sponge, **fat and pulpy as a jellyfish,** came waddling up behind her sister to see what was going on."

METAPHOR
In Chapter 2 Aunt Sponge and Aunt Spiker describe themselves and each other in the form of a poem. In the following excerpt, Aunt Sponge is describing Aunt Spiker, who is lean and tall and bony.

" '**My dear old trout!**' Aunt Sponge cried out,
'You're only bones and skin!' "

Notice that in this case, it is a metaphor because Aunt Spiker is said to *be* a trout and not just *like* a trout.

Unlikely Comparisons

Find the simile or metaphor in each example. Then tell which it is and which unlike things are being compared. Then give the reason for the comparison.

1. From *The Great Gilly Hopkins,* by Katherine Paterson ("Sarsparilla to Sorcery")
Situation: Gilly thinks back to when she was in first grade.

"The minute that … teacher had told Mrs. Dixon that she was afraid Gilly might be 'slow,' Gilly had determined to make the old parrot choke on her crackers. And she had. By Christmastime she was reading circles around the whole snotty class."

_____ is a _____.

_____

_____

_____

2. From *Because of Winn Dixie,* by Kate DiCamillo (Chapter 1)
Situation: Opal is checking over the dog who has followed her out of the Winn Dixie store.

"Mostly, he looked like a big piece of old brown carpet that had been left out in the rain."

_____ is a _____.

_____

_____

_____

3. From *The Jungle Book,* by Rudyard Kipling
Situation: Shere Kahn, the tiger, wants the wolves to give him the man's cub.

"Mother Wolf shook herself clear of the cubs and sprang forward, her eyes, like two green moons in the darkness, facing the blazing eyes of Shere Kahn."

_____ is a _____.

_____

_____

_____

Unlikely Comparisons, Continued

4. From *Charlotte's Web,* by E.B. White (Chapter XI, "The Miracle")
Situation: The narrator was describing how Charlotte's web looked on a foggy morning.

"This morning each thin strand was decorated with dozens of tiny beads of water. The web glistened in the light and made a pattern of loveliness and mystery, like a delicate veil."

_____ is a _____.

_____

_____

_____

5. From *Flora & Ulysses,* by Kate DiCamillo (Chapter Fifty-nine, "Destination Unknown")
Situation: Flora is thinking about William Spiver. Flora's mother has taken Ulysses (a squirrel) and Flora had hoped William Spiver would have been more helpful in finding him.

"Why had she thought of him as her port in a storm? Was it because ... she couldn't give up on the idea that he might say something ... helpful?"

_____ is a _____.

_____

_____

_____

6. From *Tuck Everlasting,* by Natalie Babbitt (Chapter 12)
Situation: The author first describes the sky and its reflection and then the setting sun.

"The sky was a ragged blaze of red and pink and orange, and its double trembled on the surface of the pond like color spilled from a paintbox. The sun was dropping fast now, a soft red sliding egg yolk."

_____ is a _____.

_____

_____ is a _____.

_____

_____

Creative Comparisons

Part One: Complete these sentences using a simile or a metaphor. Then tell whether it is a simile or a metaphor.

1. Situation: Maria is shopping with her mother. She comes out of the dressing room wearing a long yellow dress with brown spots that her mother has insisted she try on.

Maria says, "_____

_____"

2. Situation: Zack is on his hands and knees. His little cousin Rebecca is sitting on his back. Zack's mother walks in and sees them.

Zack's mother says, "_____

_____

3. Situation: Connor thinks his little brother Greg gets away with a lot by being deceitful.

Connor says to his mother, "_____

_____"

Part Two: Rewrite the phrases in bold using a metaphor.

4. "My **little boy has too much food in his mouth,**" Julio's mother exclaimed when she saw that his cheeks were bulging with food.

_____

_____

5. Emma swung from bar to bar. "Wow! Look at **my daughter** go!" shouted her father with pride.

_____

_____

6. Jake and his friends have been in the pool for hours. Jake's father says to them, "It's time for **you boys** to get out of the water."

_____

_____

Allusion

Allusion is a reference to something outside the work in which it is found. Allusion is sometimes metaphorical. For example, an author might describe a difficult task by writing, "It was a Herculean task."

EXAMPLES FROM LITERATURE:

From *Bud, Not Buddy,* by Christopher Paul Curtis (Chapter 3)

Situation #1: Bud as narrator describes how he battled what he thought was a vampire bat in the shed.

"I raised the rake over my head again, closed my eyes and swung it like I was **Paul Bunyan** chopping down a tree with one blow."

The allusion is to Paul Bunyan, an American folk hero. Paul Bunyan was a lumberjack and he symbolized strength, the willingness to work hard, and the creativity to overcome all obstacles.

Situation #2: Bud now realizes that what he thought was a vampire bat was really a hornet's nest.

"This time when I charged at the door I put my hand out like **Paul Robeson** running down the football field."

The allusion is to Paul Robeson. In addition to being a civil-rights activist and a singer, Paul Robeson was an outstanding football player while in college. The allusion refers to his running skills.

Statue of Paul Bunyan in Bangor, Maine
Photographer: Dennis Jarvis

Paul Robeson
(Source: Library of Congress)

It's an Allusion

Identify and explain the allusion in each excerpt.

1. From *The Great Gilly Hopkins,* by Katherine Paterson ("William Ernest and Other Mean Flowers")
Situation: Agnes has been trying to befriend Gilly, but Gilly has been ignoring her. When Agnes offers Gilly some gum, Gilly hesitates and then accepts.

"Oh, what the heck. The queen had used Rumpelstiltskin, hadn't she? Agnes might come in handy some day."

_____

_____

_____

2. From *Anastasia Krupnik,* by Lois Lowry (Chapter 2)
Situation: Anastasia's parents have told her that her mother is expecting a baby.

" 'What are you trying to do, be in the *Guinness Book of World Records?'* she asked her mother. 'You're too old to have a baby!' "

_____

_____

_____

3. From *Treasure Island,* by Robert Louis Stevenson (Chapter 10, "The Voyage")
Situation: Jim Hawkins is describing the crew of the *Hispaniola.*

"Every man on board seemed well content, and they must have been hard to please if they had been otherwise; for it is my belief there was never a ship's company so spoiled since Noah put to sea."

_____

_____

_____

Allusions as Context Clues

For each, use the allusion to help you choose the correct word or phrase to complete the sentence.

1. Suzanna was very proud of her brother Nick; he was a real Thomas Edison.

    Nick was an _____.

                    a. artist   b. inventor   c. author

2. Sara thought that the new boy in her class was quite an Adonis.

    He was very _____.

                    a. handsome   b. smart   c. wealthy

3. Juan told his sister that she was being a grinch.

    He thought that his sister was being _____.

                    a. stupid   b. helpful   c. mean spirited

4. Sophia called her brother a good samaritan.

    Sophia thought her brother was _____.

                    a. smart   b. generous   c. helpful

5. Jackson agreed to clean out the garage; he knew it would be a Herculean task.

    He knew the task would be _____.

                    a. worthwhile   b. difficult   c. enjoyable

6. When Liam told his version of what had happened, his sister looked to see if his nose had grown like Pinocchio's.

    Liam's sister thought his version was _____.

                    a. the truth   b. funny   c. a lie

A Biographical Sketch

Write a paragraph describing someone. The person may or may not be famous. Your sketch may even be autobiographical! Use an allusion in your opening sentence. Your details should support that allusion.

You may allude to one of the following people or characters, or you may choose one of your own.

Possible Suggestions for Your Allusion

The Grinch

Superman

Good Samaritan

Wonder Woman

Dr. Seuss

Pinocchio

Jack from Jack & Jill

Peter Pan

Santa Claus

Dr. Seuss

_____

_____

_____

_____

_____

_____

_____

_____

_____

_____

_____

_____

_____

Personification

Personification is the giving of human qualities to inanimate objects, ideas, or animals. These qualities include thoughts, feelings, and actions.

EXAMPLES FROM LITERATURE:

From *Out of the Dust,* by Karen Hesse

Out of the Dust contains excellent examples of personification. Set in Oklahoma in the 1930s, the book is in the form of a young girl's journal. It gives readers great insight into what it was like to live during the terrible dust storms of that time period. The personification (indicated in bold) of the wheat, the snow, the land, and especially the rain in these excerpts makes their importance even more apparent.

"The winter wheat … **stood helpless.**"
(March 1934)
"Snow … **soothed** the **parched lips** of the land." (May 1935)
"It was the **kindest** kind of rain that fell."
(May 1935)
"[The rain] kept coming … **dancing** from the heavens." (May 1935)

From *Heidi,* by Johanna Spyri (Chapter 3 "A Day with the Goats")

Heidi has spent the day up on the pasture with Peter, the goatherd. When she returns at the end of the day, Grandfather asks her if she enjoyed herself.

" 'Oh yes,' she cried, and told him all the wonderful things that happened during the day. 'The fire in the evening was the best of all. Peter said it wasn't a fire, but he couldn't tell me what it really was. You can though, Grandfather, can't you?' "

" 'It's the **sun's way of saying goodnight to the mountains**,' he explained. '**He** spreads that beautiful light over them **so that they won't forget him** till **he** comes back in the morning.' "

The sun is being personified by having it saying goodnight and referring to it as *he* and *him*. The mountains are also personified by saying they won't forget the sun. Can you figure out what event Grandfather is describing?

How Humanlike!

For each excerpt tell what is being personified and how it is personified. Be sure to include the word or words that are most important to the personification in your explanation.

1. From *Shiloh,* by Phyllis Reynolds Naylor (Chapter 6)

"I stare into the darkness of the living room and the darkness stares back."

_____

_____

_____

2. From *Tuck Everlasting,* by Natalie Babbitt (Chapter 1)

"[The road] widened and seemed to pause. ... And then it went on again and came at last to the wood. ... But on reaching the shadows of the first trees, it veered sharply, swung out in a wide arc as if, for the first time, it had reason to think where it was going, and passed around."

_____

_____

_____

3. From *Through the Looking Glass,* by Lewis Carroll (Chapter 1, "Looking-Glass House")

" 'I wonder if the snow loves the trees and fields, that it kisses them so gently? And then it covers them up snug, you know, with a white quilt; and perhaps it says 'Go to sleep, darlings, till the summer comes again.' "

_____

_____

_____

4. From *The House of Dies Drear,* by Virginia Hamilton (Chapter 3)

"The house has secrets! Thomas admired the house for keeping them so long."

_____

_____

_____

How Humanlike! Continued

5. From *The Wind in the Willows,* by Kenneth Grahame (Chapter 1)

"The Mole was bewitched, entranced, fascinated. By the side of the river he trotted as one trots, when very small, by the side of a man who holds one spell-bound by exciting stories; and when tired at last, he sat on the bank, while the river still chattered on to him, a babbling procession of the best stories in the world, sent from the heart of the earth to be told at last to the insatiable sea."

_____

_____

_____

6. From *The Phantom Tollbooth,* by Norton Juster (Chapter 3)

"For an instant there was an ominous stillness, quieter and more silent than ever before, as if even the air was holding its breath."

_____

_____

_____

7. From *A Year Down Yonder,* by Richard Peck ("Vittles and Vengeance")

"It was so quiet, you could hear Bootsie chew, and from miles away came the mournful whistle of a freight train."

_____

_____

_____

8. From *Anne of Green Gables,* by L.M. Montgomery ("Morning at Green Gables)
Anne is describing to Marilla the beauty of the day.

" 'Don't you just feel as if you just loved the world on a morning like this? And I can hear the brook laughing all the way up here. Have you ever noticed what cheerful things brooks are? They're always laughing. Even in wintertime I've heard them under the ice.' "

_____

_____

_____

Personification Sentences

For each item write a sentence in which you give the object or idea human qualities. You may make the nouns plural if you wish.

1. an airplane: _____

_____

_____

2. a rose: _____

_____

_____

3. the sun: _____

_____

_____

4. the moon: _____

_____

_____

5. a river: _____

_____

_____

6. a mountain: _____

_____

_____

7. a summer breeze: _____

_____

_____

8. a railroad train: _____

_____

_____

Educational Books 'n' Bingo

Figurative Language & Other Literary Devices, 3–6

Anthropomorphism

Anthropomorphism, which is sometimes confused with personification, is when animals or inanimate objects are portrayed as people. It is not the same as personification. For example, in *Mrs. Frisby and the Rats of NIMH,* written by Robert C. O'Brien, most of the characters are mice or rats. This is an example of anthropomorphism; it is not personification.

For each, tell whether the excerpt is an example of personification or anthropomorphism.

1. From *The Jungle Book,* by Rudyard Kipling ("Mowglie's Brothers")

"Father Wolf listened, and below in the valley that ran down to a little river, he heard the dry, angry, singsong whine of a tiger who has caught nothing and does not care if all the jungle knows it."

This excerpt is an example of _____.

2. From *The Wind in the Willows,* by Kenneth Grahame (Chapter 1, "The River Bank")

" 'I beg your pardon,' said the Mole, pulling himself together with an effort. 'You must think me very rude; but all this is so new to me. So—this—is—a—River!' "

This excerpt is an example of _____.

3. From *Tuck Everlasting,* by Natalie Babbitt (Chapter 17)

"The first week of August was reasserting itself after a good night's sleep."

This excerpt is an example of _____.

4. From *The Tale of Despereaux,* by Kate DiCamillo (Chapter Eighteen, "Confessions")

" 'I am,' said Roscuro, 'exactly that—a rat. Allow me to congratulate you on your very astute powers of observation.' "

This excerpt is an example of _____.

5. From *Charlotte's Web,* by E.B. White (Chapter V, "Charlotte")

" 'Well, I *am* pretty,' replied Charlotte. 'There's no denying that. Almost all spiders are rather nice looking.' "

This excerpt is an example of _____.

Hyperbole

Hyperbole is a deliberate exaggeration. Hyperbole can be used to create a mood, to emphasize a fact, or to add humor.

Examples of Hyperbole

I'm so hungry, I could eat a horse.

There were a million people at the party.

I think I just gained fifty pounds after eating this huge dinner.

I must have a thousand mosquito bites.

It will take a year to clean this closet!

EXAMPLE FROM LITERATURE:

Anne of Green Gables, by L.M. Montgomery
In the chapter entitled "Anne's Apology," Anne must apologize for her rude behavior—behavior she does not truly regret. She uses hyperbole in her apology.

" 'Oh, Mrs. Lynde, I am so extremely sorry,' she said with a quiver in her voice. 'I could never express all my sorrow, no, not if I used up a whole dictionary. You must just imagine it. I behaved terribly to you—and I've disgraced the dear friends, Matthew and Marilla, who have let me stay at Green Gables although I'm not a boy. I'm a dreadfully wicked and ungrateful girl, and I deserve to be punished and cast out by respectable people forever. It was very wicked of me to fly into a temper because you told me the truth. It *was* the truth; every word you said was true. My hair is red and I'm freckled and skinny and ugly. What I said to you was true, too, but I shouldn't have said it. Oh, Mrs. Lynde, please, please, forgive me. If you refuse it will be a lifelong sorrow to me. You wouldn't like to inflict a lifelong sorrow on a poor little orphan girl, would you, even if she had a dreadful temper? Oh, I am sure you wouldn't. Please say you forgive me, Mrs. Lynde.' "

Don't Exaggerate!

Underline the hyperbole in each excerpt. Then rewrite the underlined portion without using hyperbole. Make changes to eliminate the hyperbole without changing the meanings.

1. From *Shiloh,* by Phyllis Reynolds Naylor (Chapter 1)
Situation: The family has just eaten a large meal.
" The best thing about Sundays is we eat our big meal at noon. Once you get your belly full, you can walk all over West Virginia before you're hungry again."

_____

_____

2. From *Because of Winn Dixie,* by Kate DiCamillo (Chapter 7)
Situation: Miss Franny Block, the librarian, is telling Opal about her childhood.
" 'Back when Florida was wild, when it consisted of nothing but palmetto trees and mosquitos so big they could fly away with you … my father told me that I could have anything I wanted for my birthday.' "

_____

_____

3. From *Diary of a Wimpy Kid: The Long Haul,* by Jeff Kinney
Situation: Greg Heffley and his family are at Soak Central, a water park.
"We went to the giant pool first, but there were about a BILLION people in it."

_____

_____

4. From *A Year Down Yonder,* by Richard Peck ("A Minute in the Morning")
Situation: Mary Alice occasionally heard noises coming from the attic above her.
"I didn't think Grandma's house was haunted. What ghost would dare? But she slept downstairs to spare herself the climb, so I was miles from anybody."

_____

_____

Johnny Appleseed

Hyperbole is an essential part of tall tales. John Chapman, better known as Johnny Appleseed, was very important to early settlers of the Midwest. This pioneer nurseryman introduced apple trees to large areas of Pennsylvania, Ohio, Indiana, and Illinois, and parts of what is today West Virginia. Tall tales and legends about him spread. For each statement decide whether or not hyperbole is being used and circle TRUTH or EXAGGERATION.

1. John Chapman was born in Massachusetts in 1774. He died in 1845.

   TRUTH / EXAGGERATION

2. John Chapman's first nursery was planted on land given to him for being a soldier during the Revolutionary War.

   TRUTH / EXAGGERATION

3. He earned the nickname by developing apple nurseries throughout the countryside.

   TRUTH / EXAGGERATION

4. He never wore shoes and even walked barefoot over ice. The skin on his feet was so thick that even a rattlesnake couldn't bite through it.

   TRUTH / EXAGGERATION

5. His only clothing consisted of coffee sacks with holes cut out for his arms.

   TRUTH / EXAGGERATION

6. He often traded food or clothing for his apple trees.

   TRUTH / EXAGGERATION

From Howe's Historical
Collections of Ohio,
Centennial Edition, 1903

JOHNNY APPLESEED.

7. He always wore a heavy metal pot on his head instead of a hat.

   TRUTH / EXAGGERATION

8. He almost always carried a leather bag filled with apple seeds.

   TRUTH / EXAGGERATION

9. He never killed animals.

   TRUTH / EXAGGERATION

10. Beginning in 1792, he planted apple trees farther and farther west.

   TRUTH / EXAGGERATION

Creating Hyperbole

We all use hyperbole from time to time. Write a sentence for each situation using hyperbole, or overstatement.

1. Situation: You have just come home from school after having to skip lunch.

_____

_____

2. Situation: You just got back from the movies. Your friend has asked how you liked it.

_____

_____

3. Situation: You are watching a new TV show.

_____

_____

4. Situation: You have just gotten back from a three-week journey.

_____

_____

5. Situation: It is a very hot day.

_____

_____

6. Situation: It is a very cold day.

_____

_____

7. Situation: Your teacher has given you a lot of homework.

_____

_____

8. Situation: You have just jumped into a swimming pool.

_____

_____

Understatement

Understatement is the opposite of hyperbole. Like hyperbole, it can be serious or funny.

EXAMPLES FROM LITERATURE:

Robinson Crusoe, by Daniel DeFoe
Early in *Robinson Crusoe,* in the chapter entitled "The Storm," Robinson Crusoe's companion asks him after a strong storm if he was frightened by the "capful of wind."

The understatement has the effect of trivializing the main character's belief that it was a terrible storm.

From *Charlie and the Chocolate Factory,* by Roald Dahl

Read each excerpt and explain the understatement.

1. In Chapter 17 Augustus Gloop ignored Mr. Wonka's warnings and fell into the chocolate river. He has been sucked into a glass pipe. The others are watching the chocolate swishing around him when he suddenly disappears.

" 'Call the fire brigade!' yelled Mrs. Gloop.
'Keep calm!' cried Mr. Wonka. ... 'Augustus has gone on a little journey, that's all.' "

_____

_____

_____

2. In Chapter 21 Violet turns purple from head to toe after chewing a piece of gum that Mr. Wonka has warned her not to eat.

" 'I would rather you didn't take it,' Mr. Wonka warned her gently. 'You see, I haven't got it *quite right* yet.' "

_____

_____

_____

More Understatement

A **litote** is a special kind of understatement. It uses a negative statement to state a positive idea.
To describe a good artist, you might say, "He's not a bad artist."
To describe a driver who has had many accidents, you might say, "He's not the greatest driver."

EXAMPLES FROM LITERATURE:

The View from Saturday, by E.L. Konigsburg ("Julian Narrates When Ginger Played Annie's Sandy")
Michael Froelich's dog Arnold was an understudy for Nadia's dog Ginger. Nadia did not trust Michael and was afraid he would do something to harm Ginger.

"During the actual performances [Michael] and Arnold were to stay backstage and out of sight— unless something happened to Ginger. ... I was not without worry."

Identify the litote and rewrite the sentence without the litote.

_____

_____

A Long Way from Chicago, by Richard Peck ("Shotgun Cheatham's Last Night Above Ground")
A reporter was asking questions about Shotgun Cheatham, who had just died.

"Grandma had already heard it on the grapevine that Shotgun was no more, though she wasn't the first person people ran to with news. She wasn't what you'd call a popular woman."

Identify the litote and rewrite the sentence without the litote.

_____

_____

Write a phrase to describe each subject using understatement.

1. A Football Stadium During the Super Bowl _____

2. A 5,000-Passenger Cruise Ship _____

3. A Tornado _____

4. Mount Rushmore _____

5. The Grand Canyon _____

Oxymora

An **oxymoron** is a phrase made up of seemingly contradictory terms—terms that don't seem to go together. Originally, the word *oxymoron* was used to describe only the deliberate joining of contradictory terms for effect, such as "deafening silence." Today it is commonly used to describe terms that are based on alternate meanings of a word or words, such as "jumbo shrimp." The plural of *oxymoron* is *oxymora*, which is preferred, or *oxymorons*.

Examples of Oxymora

act naturally
active retirement
almost exactly
anxious patient
burning cold
cautiously optimistic
deafening silence
definite maybe
icy hot
jumbo shrimp
larger half
minor catastrophe
old news
only choice
organized chaos
original copy
partial silence
partial success
random order
small crowd
sweet sorrow
tough love
unbiased opinion
virtual reality
working vacation

EXAMPLE FROM LITERATURE:

Romeo and Juliet, by William Shakespeare
One of the most famous oxymora is from Act 2, Scene 2 of William Shakespeare's *Romeo and Juliet* when Juliet says good night.
"Good night, good night! Parting is such sweet sorrow."
"Sweet sorrow" is an oxymoron.

Working with Oxymora

1. Identify and explain the oxymora in the following excerpts from *The Phantom Tollbooth,* by Norton Juster (Chapter 10, "A Colorful Symphony")

Situation: Milo goes to each door of the small house and is greeted at each by a man. Each describes himself:

Man No. 1 said, "I'm the smallest giant in the world."

Man No. 2 said, "I'm the tallest midget in the world."

Man No. 3 said that he was "the thinnest fat man in the world."

Man No. 4 said that he was "the fattest thin man in the world."

_____

_____

_____

_____

2. From *Romeo and Juliet,* by William Shakespeare
In addition to "sweet sorrow," given in the example, *Romeo and Juliet* has many examples of oxymora. Read the lines from Act 1, Scene 1 and circle the oxymora.

"Why then, O brawling love! O loving hate!
O any thing, of nothing first create!
O heavy lightness, serious vanity,
Misshapen chaos of well-seeming forms,
Feather of lead, bright smoke, cold fire, sick health,
Still-waking sleep, that is not what it is!"

Create three original sentences using oxymora. You may choose from the list on the previous page, or you may create your own.

_____

_____

_____

_____

_____

_____

_____

_____

Symbols

Authors sometimes use **symbols** to express a theme. An object, person, or event stands for an abstract idea or feeling. That symbol will have not only its real, concrete meaning but also its symbolic meaning. Some symbols are universally recognized; examples are a heart for love, a skull for death, and a flag for patriotism. Other symbols are created for a particular work.

EXAMPLE FROM LITERATURE:

From *Robinson Crusoe,* by Daniel Defoe ("A Footprint")
BACKGROUND INFORMATION: Robinson Crusoe has been stranded on a deserted island. He has been alone for many years and has seen no hint that another human being could be on the island. After all these years, he is shocked to see a footprint in the sand.

"It happened one day about noon going toward my boat, I was exceedingly surprised with the print of a man's naked foot on the shore, which was very plain to be seen in the sand.
. . . .
To have seen one of my own species would have seemed to me a raising me from death to life, and the greatest blessing that Heaven itself, next to the supreme blessing of salvation, could bestow; I say, that I should now tremble at the very apprehensions of seeing a man, and was ready to sink into the ground at but the shadow or silent appearance of a man's having set his foot in the island."

The footprint represents Robinson Crusoe's mixed feelings about companionship and about the prospect of rejoining human society. He used to long for these things, but now he also fears them.

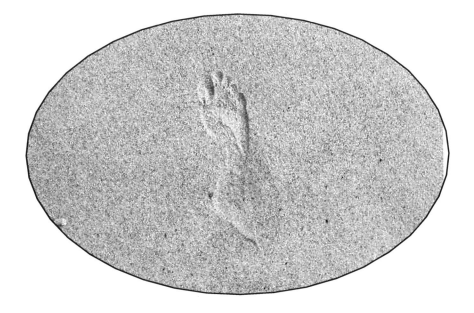

Symbolism in Tuck Everlasting

Tuck Everlasting, by Natalie Babbitt, is the story of ten-year-old Winnie Foster and her encounter with the Tuck family, doomed to eternal life after drinking from a magic spring. The novel contains many symbols. Read the excerpts and answer the questions.

1. Chapter 3: It is before Winnie has met the Tucks. She is feeling as if her parents are always telling her what to do. She sees a toad nearby and tells her thoughts about wanting to be on her own to the toad.

" 'And I might even decide to have a pet. Maybe a big old toad, like you, that I could keep in a nice cage ...' At this the toad ... plopped its heavy mudball of a body a few inches farther away from her. 'I suppose you're right,' said Winnie. 'Then you'd be just the way I am, now. ... It would be better if I could be like you, out in the open and making up my own mind.' "

What might the toad represent?

_____

_____

2. Chapter 12: Tuck has just explained the water cycle to Winnie.

" 'It's a wheel, Winnie. Everything's a wheel, turning and turning, never stopping. The frogs is part of it, and the bugs, and the fish, and the wood thrush, too. And people. But never the same ones. ... That's the way it's supposed to be.' "

" 'We ain't part of the wheel anymore.' "

" 'But dying's part of the wheel, right there next to being born.' "

" 'If I knowed how to climb back on the wheel, I'd do it in a minute.' "

What is the symbol in these excerpts? What does it represent?

_____

_____

2. Chapter 22: Jesse Tuck has given a bottle of the magic spring water to Winnie.

" 'You keep it. And then, no matter where you are, when you're seventeen, Winnie you can drink it, and then come find us.' "

What might the bottle of water represent?

_____

_____

So Many Symbols

Suppose you were writing a novel. What symbols might you use to represent various concepts?

OUR COUNTRY

LOVE

PEACE

WAR

BEAUTY

FREEDOM

INNOCENCE

PASSAGE OF TIME

EVIL

GOOD LUCK

Puns

A **pun** is a play on words. Most puns are based upon different meanings of the same word or on different words with similar pronunciations. Puns are usually, but not always, humorous.

EXAMPLE FROM LITERATURE:

The Phantom Toll Booth, by Norton Juster (Chapter 2, "Beyond Expectations")
Situation: The Whether Man has asked Milo if it will rain.

Milo responds, " 'I thought you were the Weather Man.' "
The Whether Man then explains, " 'Oh no, I'm the Whether Man, for after all it's more important to know whether there will be weather than what the weather will be.' "

The pun is based on the two words which are pronounced in the same way but have different meanings: *weather* and *whether.*

Identify and Explain

Identify and explain the pun in the following excerpts.

1. From *The Phantom Toll Booth,* by Norton Juster (Chapter 2, "Beyond Expectations")
Situation: Milo has been charged with various offenses.

The police officer, who is also the judge, asks Milo, " 'Would you like a long or short sentence?' "
Milo responds, " 'A short one if you please.' "
The judge then says, " 'Good, I always have trouble remembering the long ones. How about *I am*? That's the shortest sentence I know.' "

_____

_____

_____

2. From *Charlie and the Chocolate Factory,* by Roald Dahl (Chapter 18)
Situation: Mr. Wonka has just explained the whips found in the storeroom are for whipping cream and goes on to explain about poached eggs.

"A poached egg isn't a poached egg unless it's been stolen from the woods in the dead of night."

_____

_____

_____

Devices of Sound: Alliteration

Some literary devices rely on sound. **Alliteration** is one such device. It is the repetition of initial consonant sounds. Alliteration not only adds a poetic sound, it also helps emphasize the phrases.

EXAMPLE FROM LITERATURE:

From *The Great Gilly Hopkins,* by Katherine Paterson ("Sarsaparilla to Sorcery")
Situation: Gilly is imagining what it would be like if her mother came and got her.
" 'I'd turn from **gruesome Gilly** into **gorgeous, gracious, good, glorious Galadriel.** And **grateful**—I'd be so **grateful!**' "

The alliterative words are in bold.

Alliteration Search
Find the alliteration in these excerpts. Circle the alliterative words.

1. From *Charlie and the Chocolate Factory,* by Roald Dahl (Chapter 6)
There is a description of Augustus Gloop as he appeared in the newspaper article when he found the golden ticket:

"The picture showed a nine-year-old boy who was so enormously fat he looked as though he had been blown up with a powerful pump. Great flabby folds of fat bulged out from every part of his body, and his face was like a monstrous ball of dough with two small greedy curranty eyes peering out upon the world. ... Flags were flying from all the windows, children had been given a holiday from school, and a parade was being organized in honor of the famous youth."

2. From *Flora & Ulysses,* by Kate DiCamillo (Chapter Twenty-two, "A Giant Ear")
This tells about Flora's father.

"Flora's father was an accountant at the firm Flinton, Flosston, and Frick."

3. From *Diary of a Wimpy Kid: The Long Haul,* by Jeff Kinney
Greg writes about the magazine that his mother loves.

"I've flipped through 'Family Frolic' a few times, and I have to admit, the pictures make everything look like a lot of fun."

Devices of Sound: Onomatopoeia

Onomatopoeia is the use of a word that mimics the sound it represents. Some examples are *buzz, jingle, moan, meow, quack, moo, bang, click,* and *roar.* Onomatopoeia is often used in poetry.

EXAMPLES FROM LITERATURE:

The onomatopoetic words are in bold.

From *The Lightning Thief,* by Rick Riordan (1849)
Rick Riordan used many onomatopoetic words throughout the novel. The following are a few examples.

"I heard a slow ***clop-clop-clop,*** like muffled wooden blocks."

"There was a blinding flash, a jaw-rattling ***boom,*** and our car exploded."

"The monster tensed, gave a surprised **grunt,** then—***snap!***"

"***Thwack!*** At first I figured it was the sound of Grover hitting a tree. Then Medusa **roared** with rage."

"***Fump-fump-fump.*** A riverboat's paddlewheel churned about me. . . ."

"I heard it go ***ker-sploosh*** in the River Styx."

"The Moon," from *A Child's Garden of Verses,* by Robert Louis Stevenson

The moon has a face like the clock in the hall;
She shines on thieves on the garden wall
On streets and fields and harbour quays,
And birdies asleep in the forks of the trees.

The **squalling** cat and the **squeaking** mouse,
The **howling** dog by the door of the house,
The bat that lies in bed at noon,
All love to be out by the light of the moon.

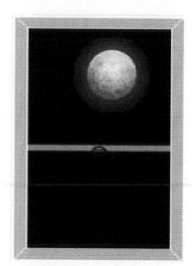

But all of the things that belong to the day
Cuddle to sleep to be out of her way,
And flowers and children close their eyes
Till up in the morning the sun shall arise.

Identifying Onomatopoeia

Look for onomatopoeia in the following excerpts. Write the onomatopoetic words and explain why they are onomatopoetic.

1. From *The Phantom Toll Booth,* by Norton Juster ("Confusion in the Market Place")
Situation: Milo is in the Market Place where words and letters are being sold.
" 'Perhaps I can be of some assistance—a-s-s-i-s-t-a-n-c-e,' buzzed an unfamiliar voice, and when Milo looked up he saw an enormous bee, at least twice his size, sitting on top of the wagon."

_____

_____

_____

2. From *The Tale of Despereaux,* by Kate DiCamillo (Chapter 6, "This Drum")
Situation: Members of the Mouse Council were being summoned.
"*Boom. Tat-tat. Boom. Tat-tat. Boom.* The beating of the drum let them know that an important decision would have to be made, one that affected the safety and well-being of the entire mouse community."

_____

_____

_____

3. From *The Tale of Despereaux,* by Kate DiCamillo (Chapter 21, "The Queen's Last Words")
Situation: A rat had fallen into the queen's bowl of soup.
"In response, the queen flung her spoon in the air and made an incredible noise, a noise that was in no way worthy of a queen, a noise somewhere between the neigh of a horse and the squeal of a pig."

_____

_____

_____

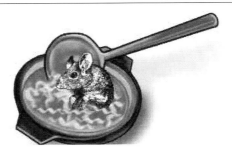

Onomatopoetic Words

The following is a list of some onomatopoetic words.

achoo	crunch	kerplunk	squeak
bang	cuckoo	knock	squeal
beep	drip	meow	squish
bong	flutter	moan	swish
boom	gong	mumble	tap
buzz	groan	murmur	tick-tock
cheep	growl	mutter	thump
chime	grunt	plop	tinkle
clang	gurgle	quack	wail
clank	hiccup	rattle	whack
clop	hiss	sizzle	wheeze
cluck	honk	slurp	whisper
crackle	howl	sob	whoosh
crash	hum	splash	yelp
creak	jingle	splat	zip

See how many words you can add to the list!

Categorize the words:

Words Related to Water

Words Related to Collisions

Words Related to Voice

Words Related to Animal Sounds

Words Related to Moving through Air

Words Related to _____

Figurative Language & Other Literary Devices, 3–6

Educational Books 'n' Bingo

Post-Unit Activities

Post-Unit Activities

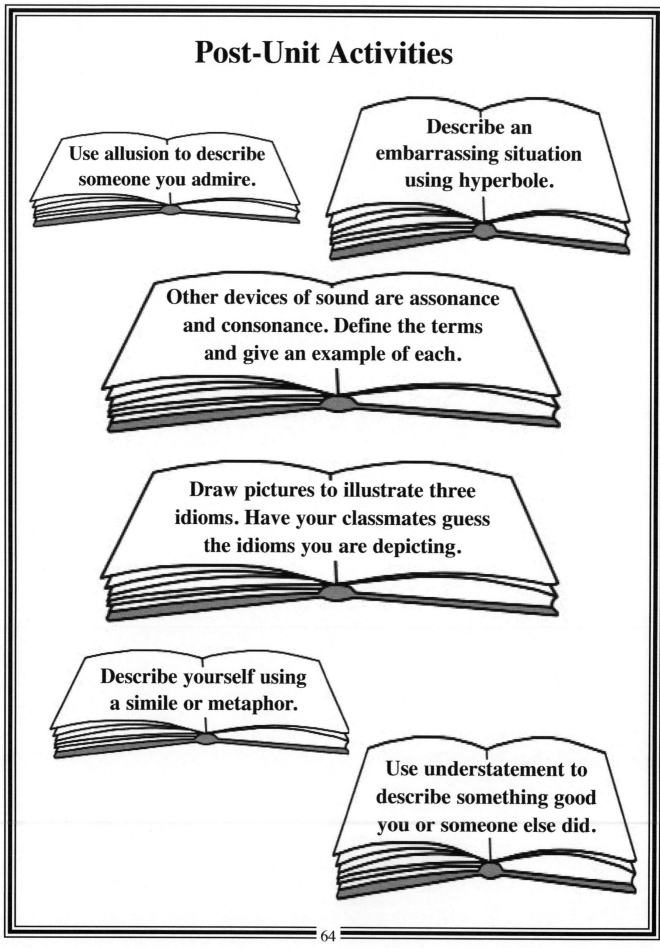

Use allusion to describe someone you admire.

Describe an embarrassing situation using hyperbole.

Other devices of sound are assonance and consonance. Define the terms and give an example of each.

Draw pictures to illustrate three idioms. Have your classmates guess the idioms you are depicting.

Describe yourself using a simile or metaphor.

Use understatement to describe something good you or someone else did.

Name the Technique

For each excerpt, identify the literary device in bold.

_____   1. From *A Year Down Yonder,* by Richard Peck

"**The ice** on the wovenwire fences **was a lattice-work of diamonds**."

_____   2. From *A Year Down Yonder,* by Richard Peck

" 'Were tornadoes worse when you were a girl?' I asked to test her. She waved me away. **'What we had today was a light breeze.'** "

_____   3. From *Flora & Ulysses,* by Kate DiCamillo

"She knew that it was ridiculous, but sometimes **she felt as if Mary Ann** [the name she had given to a lamp] **knew something** that she didn't know. ..."

_____   4. From *Holes,* by Louis Sachar

"A sign on the door said **WRECK ROOM.** Nearly everything in the room was broken."

_____   5. From *The Wind in the Willows,* by Kenneth Grahame

"Greatly alarmed, he made a grab at the side of the boat, and the next moment—**sploosh!**"

_____   6. From *Anne of Green Gables,* by L. M. Montgomery

"Below the garden a **green field lush with clover** sloped down to the hollow where the **brook ran** and where scores of **white birches** grew, **upspringing airily** out of an undergrowth....Beyond it was a hill, **green and feathery** with spruce and fir. ..."

Figurative Language & Other Literary Devices, 3–6

_____ 7. From *Anne of Green Gables,* by L. M. Montgomery

" 'For pity's sake, **hold your tongue,**' said Marilla. 'You talk entirely too much for a little girl.' **"**

_____ 8. From *Because of Winn Dixie,* by Kate DiCamillo

"Some of his fur was pretty loose and **blew right off of him like a dandelion puff."**

_____ 9. From *James and the Giant Peach,* by Roald Dahl

"She [Aunt Sponge] **was like a great white soggy overboiled cabbage."**

_____ 10. From *Because of Winn Dixie,* by Kate DiCamillo

"I could see **him** [the preacher] pulling his old **turtle head** back into his stupid **turtle shell."**

_____ 11. From *Through the Looking Glass,* by Lewis Carroll

" 'I was very nearly opening the window and putting you [a cat] out in the snow! And you'd have deserved it, you **mischievous darling!**"

_____ 12. From *Lily's Crossing,* by Patricia Reilly Giff

" 'There's enough candy here for whole army."

_____ 13. From *The Adventures of Tom Sawyer,* by Mark Twain

"Hang the boy, can't I learn anything. ... **Can't learn any old dog new tricks, as the saying is."**

_____ 14. From *Out of the Dust,* by Karen Hesse

"The winter wheat ... stood helpless."

Word Search

Find the words listed below. They may be right to left, left to right, up, down, or diagonal.

```
U N D E R S T A T E M E N T H M F B D N O
E N I E N R A S N O E P N N Y E O E E O X
N O I T A C I F I N O S R E P N O R N I Y
Y I I M A D O D O O I A L M E T T S O T M
I S U R E D I T O M E N E E R A B N T A O
E N N P H T A D I A L E C T B L A E A T R
Y G N O I T A R E T I L L A O E L V T O O
R R P E I Y H P M O M T S T L L L D I N N
E I U O A S O O H P I T E S E T S I O N N
G N N I A U O D O S I N R E A R O N O N N
A S D E L L I L E E R L O E G D F I E C O
M A T S Y M B O L I S M I D N L H S I N C
I P C D M S Y M N A S T B S F A H E C R C
```

alliteration	metaphor
allusion	onomatopoeia
connotation	oxymoron
denotation	personification
dialect	pun
hyperbole	simile
idiom	symbolism
imagery	understatement

Crossword Puzzle

ACROSS

1. Expression whose meaning cannot be taken literally

4. Giving human qualities to inanimate objects

6. Variety of a language

7. Reference to something outside the work

9. Use of something to represent something else

12. Humorous play on words

13. Words that mimic a sound

14. Comparison of two unlike things with the use of *like* or *as*

DOWN

2. Dictionary meaning of a word

3. Suggested meaning of a word

5. Repetition of initial consonant sounds

8. Exaggeration for effect

10. Comparison of two unlike things without the use of *like* or *as*

11. Language that appeals to the senses

Appendix

Glossary of Literary Terms

Adage: An old and well-known saying that expresses a general truth; a saying often in metaphorical form that embodies a common observation.

Alliteration: The repetition of initial consonant sounds in two or more consecutive or neighboring words.

Allusion: A reference to something outside the work in which it is found.

Antagonist: The opponent of the main character, or protagonist.

Anthropomorphism: When animals or inanimate objects are portrayed as people.

Character: An imaginary person in a work of fiction.

Character development: The method used by an author to develop a character.

Character trait: A distinguishing characteristic, or quality, of a character.

Characterization: The method used by the author to give readers information about a character; a description or representation of a person's qualities or peculiarities.

Climax: The moment in a story when the action reaches its greatest conflict.

Conflict: The struggle within a character, between characters, between a character and society, or between a character and a force of nature.

Connotation: The associations that are suggested or implied by a word that go beyond its dictionary meaning.

Denotation: The dictionary meaning of a word.

Dialect: A variety of a language that is distinguished from the standard form by pronunciation, grammar, and/or vocabulary.

Dialogue (dialog): Conversation between two or more characters.

Exposition: The beginning of a work of fiction; the part in which readers are given important background information.

Falling action: The action that comes after the climax and before the resolution.

Figurative language: Description of one thing in terms usually used for something else. Simile, metaphor, and personification are common examples of figurative language.

Flashback: Insertion of an earlier event into the normal chronological sequence of a narrative.

Foil: A character with traits opposite to those of the main character.

Foreshadowing: The use of clues to give readers a hint of events yet to occur.

Genre: A category of literature.

Historical fiction: Fiction represented in a setting true to the history of the time in which the story takes place.

Hyperbole: An exaggeration used for effect.

Idiom: An expression whose meaning cannot be determined by its literal expression.

Image: A mental picture.

Imagery: The use of language that appeals to the senses and produces mental images; the use of figures of speech or vivid descriptions to produce mental images.

Irony (situational): An outcome contrary to what was or might have been expected.

Irony (verbal): The use of words to express the opposite of their literal meaning.

Metaphor: A figure of speech that compares two unlike things without the use of *like* or *as*.

Mood: The feeling that the author creates for the reader.

Narrator: The voice and implied speaker who tells the story.

Onomatopoeia: The use of words that mimic the sounds they represent.

Oxymoron: A figure of speech made up of seemingly contradictory parts.

Paradox: A statement or situation that seems contradictory but reveals a truth.

Personification: The bestowing of human qualities on inanimate objects, ideas, or animals. (See the difference between personification and anthropomorphism.)

Plot: The ordered structure, or sequence, of causal events in a story.

Point of view: The perspective from which a story is told; the relation of the narrator to the story.

Protagonist: The main character.

Proverb: A brief popular saying that gives advice about how people should live or that expresses a belief that is generally thought to be true.

Pun: A humorous play on words that are similar in sound but different in meaning.

Realistic fiction: True-to-life fiction; people, places, and happenings are similar to those in real life.

Resolution: The part of the plot where the main dramatic conflict is worked out; the plot may or may not have a happy ending. (Also called denouement.)

Rising action: Events in a plot that occur after the exposition but before the climax.

Sarcasm: A form of verbal irony in which a person says the opposite of what he or she means.

Sequencing: The placement of story elements in a narrative order, usually chronological.

Setting: The time and place in which the main story events occur.

Simile: A figure of speech that clearly compares two unlike things through the use of *like* or *as*.

Stereotype: A character whose personality traits represent a group rather than an individual.

Style: The author's manner of writing, including grammatical structures, type of vocabulary, and the use of figurative language and other literary techniques.

Suspense: Quality that causes readers to wonder what will happen next; apprehension about what will happen.

Symbolism: The use of an object, character, or idea to represent something else.

Theme: The main idea of a literary work; the message the author wants to convey.

Tone: The attitude of the author towards his or her writing.

Understatement: To state something less strongly than the facts would indicate.

ANSWERS

(Answers may vary. Some answers call for creative thinking and are not given here.)

Connotation and Negative Connotations (Pages 12–13)

EXAMPLE: Most will probably say that *peculiar* makes them think it tasted bad. They may say that *unusual* is neutral and *out-of-the-ordinary* is positive. Students will likely circle following words: *shack, scrawny, chore, interrogate, stench, trudge, cheap, outlandish, babble, mock, snoopy,* and *withdrawn.* Accept other supported answers.

Dialogue: What's the Purpose? (Page 16)

1. It tells us that Grandfather lives on a mountain and that he is somewhat of a recluse. We also know that he used to go to church, but now he does not. People are wary of him.
2. The dialogue tells readers that the story is set in Colonial Connecticut. We also know that Kit is travelling alone and that she has travelled far.

Dialogue in Charlotte's Web (Page 17)

1. We learn that the story is set on a farm.
2. We learn that Fern loves animals and that she is a sensitive, caring person. We also see that she stands up for what she believes when it is important to her.
3. We see that Mr. Arable has an open mind. He allows Fern to try to raise the pig although he does not seem to think it is a good idea. Also, he seems to be a loving father.
4. Answers will vary, but perhaps he thought it would be good for Fern to see for herself how difficult the task was instead of just forbidding her to do it.

Interpreting Dialect (Page 20) Answers will vary. Suggestions are given.

1. In this region people rarely state the purpose for their visit right away. They greet each other and carry on a conversation first. Then they talk about the purpose of the visit.
2. People have been leaving food for me in their mailboxes. In the past, Mrs. Ellison left me banana bread, but today I found a ham sandwich.
3. Steady Eddie said, "Take a seat."

Imagery: Chart the Images (Page 24) Answers will vary. Suggestions are given. Some can go in more than one category.

SIGHT: splashes of whitewash, black fur, little paws, sunlight, great meadow, well-worn red brick, fire of logs, light

SOUND: muttering, pop!, carol of happy birds, shout, clink of plates

TOUCH: dust in his throat and eyes, aching back, weary arms, warm grass, sunshine, hot on his fur, soft breezes, caressed his heated brow, toast themselves at the fire, wet coats, warm water, warmth, warm and dry, weary legs, cold

SMELL OR TASTE: ham, dried herbs, nets of onions, basket of eggs

ACTIONS: scrooged, scrabbled, scraped, working busily, rolling, jumping off, thrust

Working with Idioms (Page 28) Answers will vary. Suggestions are given.

1. As he sat on the grass and looked across the river, he noticed a dark hole in the bank. ...
2. He said he would phone in about a week and told me to stay out of trouble.
3. And be careful. I need that saxophone to earn a living.

Some Common Idioms (Page 29) Answers will vary, but the following are some possibilities.

to get off on the wrong foot	to be all bark and no bite	to be in the bag
to be a drop in the bucket	to have an axe to grind	to be on pins and needles
to be a piece of cake	to beat around the bush	to add fuel to the fire
to be in hot water	to cost an arm and a leg	to get a kick out of

Guess the Idiom (Pages 30–31)

1. green thumb
2. at the end of my rope
3. cooking up a storm
4. hold your tongue

5. chips off the old block
6. put on her face
7. in the same boat

Similes and Metaphors: Unlikely Comparisons (Pages 35–36)

1. Calling Mrs. Dixon a parrot is a metaphor. Gilly compares her first-grade teacher to a parrot without the use of *like* or *as*. It is not specifically said, but perhaps she called her a parrot because she spoke without thinking.

2. Comparing William Spiver to a port in a storm is a simile because the word *as* is used to make the comparison. She thought of him as someone who would provide a safe haven—one who would keep her out of danger..

3. Comparing Mother Wolf's eyes to green moons is a simile. The author used *like* to make the comparison. The comparison was made because of the way Mother Wolf's eyes shined in the darkness while she was facing the tiger.

4. The web was compared to a delicate veil because of the way the drops of water made it look. It is a simile because the author used *like* to make the comparison.

5. The comparison of Mae to a great potato is a metaphor. The author says she *is* a potato, not that she looks like one.

6. The first comparison is a simile. The author says the sky's reflection (double) looks like spilled paint. The second comparison is a metaphor. The author says the setting sun is an egg yolk. The author is describing a sunset.

Creative Comparisons (Pages 37) Answers will vary. Suggestions are given.

1. Maria says, "Mother, I look like a baby giraffe in this dress!"   simile
2. Zack's mom says, "Would either horse or rider like a snack?"   metaphor
3. Connor says to his mother, "Mom, Greg is as sly as a fox!"   simile
4. "My little hamster has too much food in his mouth!" Julio's mother exclaimed.
5. "Wow! Look at my little monkey go!"
6. Jake's father says to them, "It's time for you dolphins to get out of the water."

It's an Allusion (Pages 39)

1. Gilly alludes to Rumpelstiltskin because the queen in the fairy tale used Rumpelstiltskin to try to get what she wanted and Gilly thinks she may be able to use Agnes to get what she wants.

2. Anastasia refers to the *Guinness Book of World Records* because she thinks her mother is much too old to have a baby.

3. The allusion is the reference to Noah, a biblical figure.

Allusions as Context Clues (Page 40)
1. inventor   3. mean spirited   5. difficult
2. handsome   4. helpful

Personification (Page 42)
1. He is describing a sunset.

How Humanlike! (Pages 43–44)
1. Darkness is personified because it is said to be staring.
2. The road is personified. It seemed to pause. It seemed to have the ability to think.
3. The snow is personified because it is said to love the trees and fields and tucks them in.
4. The house is personified by saying that it keeps secrets.
5. The river is personified. It chattered and told stories. The earth is personified by saying it has a heart. The sea is personified by saying it is insatiable.
(The Mole is not personified. This is anthropomorphism, which is explained next.)
6. The air is personified by saying it held its breath.
7. The train is personified by calling its whistle mournful.
8. Brooks are personified by saying they laugh and are cheerful.

Anthropomorphism (Page 46)
1. Numbers 1, 2, 4, and 5 are anthropomorphism. Number 3 is personification.

Don't Exaggerate (Page 48) Answers will vary. Suggestions are given.
1. When you finish eating, it will be a long time before you are hungry again.
2. It consisted of nothing but palmetto trees and huge mosquitos.
The fact that it consisted of nothing but palmetto trees and mosquitos is also hyperbole.
(Some might say that the fact that she could have anything she wanted was hyperbole.)
3. We went to the giant pool first, but it was very crowded.
4. But she slept downstairs, so I was not very near anyone.

Johnny Appleseed (Page 49)
1. truth   3. truth   5. exaggeration   7. exaggeration   9. truth
2. truth   4. exaggeration 6. truth   8. truth   10. truth

Understatement (Page 51)
1. Travelling through a pipe with flowing chocolate would be very serious. Calling that "a little journey" is an understatement!
2. Turning the chewer purple from head to toe would suggest that the gum was far from ready. Saying that it was "not quite right" is an understatement!

More Understatement (Page 52)
1. "Not without worry" is a litote. It can be changed to "I was worried."
2. "She wasn't what you'd call a popular woman" is a litote. It can be changed to "She was an unpopular woman."

Working with Oxymora (Page 54)
1. Smallest giant, tallest midget, thinnest fat man, and fattest thin man are oxymora.
2. Brawling love, loving hate, any thing of nothing, heavy lightness, serious vanity, chaos of well-seeming forms, feather of lead, bright smoke, cold fire, sick health, still-waking sleep, and that is what is not are all oxymora.

Symbols (Page 56)
1. The toad represents Winnie's desire for independence.
2. The symbol is the wheel. It represents the normal circle of life: birth, life, and death. The Tucks are no longer part of the wheel.
3. The bottle of water represents the temptation of eternal life.

Puns (Page 58)
1. The pun is based on the two meanings of the word *sentence:* a grammatical unit and a determination of punishment.
2. The pun is based on the two meanings of the word *poached:* a cooking method and a type of stealing.

Devices of Sound: Alliteration (Page 59)
1. picture, powerful, pump, part, peering, parade
   fat, flabby, folds, fat, face, flags, flying, from, famous
2. Flora's. father, firm, Flinton, Flosston, Frick
3. flipped, Family, Frolic, few, fun

Identifying Onomatopoeia (Page 61)
1. *Buzz* is onomatopoetic. It mimics the sound a bee makes.
2. *Boom* and *tat-tat* are onomatopoetic. They mimic the sound of a drum.
3. *Neigh* and *squeal* are onomatopoetic. They mimic the sounds of a horse and a pig respectively.

Onomatopoetic Words (Page 62) Answers will vary. Categories are started. Words may go into more than one group.
Water: drip, gurgle, splash
Collisions: clank, tap, thump,
Voice: murmur, wail, hum
Animal Sounds: buzz, cluck, meow
Blowing through Air: whiz, flutter, whoosh

Name the Technique (Page 65–66)
1. simile	4. pun	7. idiom	10. metaphor	13. proverb
2. understatement	5. onomatopoeia	8. simile	11. oxymoron	14. personification
3. personification	6. imagery	9. simile	12. hyperbole	

Word Search Puzzle (Page 67)

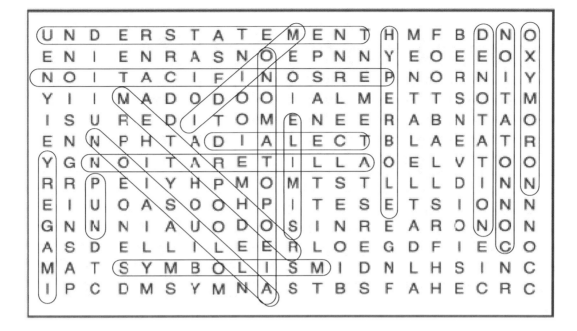

Crossword Puzzle (Page 68)

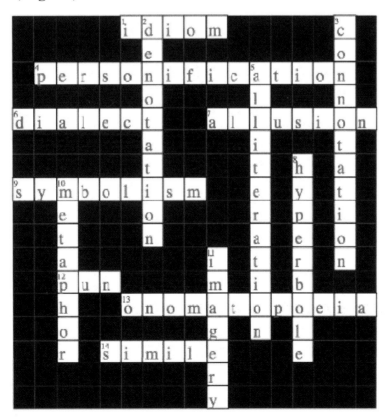

Figurative Language & Other Literary Devices, 3–6

Bibliography & Suggested Reading List

Aesop. *Library of Congress Aesop Tales*. "Aesop for Children." http://read.gov/aesop/001.html Accessed March 5, 2005.

Alcott, Louisa May. *Little Women*. New York: Penguin Group, 2004.

Babbitt, Natalie. *Tuck Everlasting*. New York: Houghton Mifflin Harcourt, 2007.

Blume, Judy. *Tales of a Fourth Grade Nothing*. New York: Dell Publishing, 1972.

Carroll, Lewis. *Alice's Adventures in Wonderland & Through the Looking-Glass*. New York Bantam Classic, 1984.

Cleary, Beverly. *Dear Mr. Henshaw*. New York: HarperCollins, 1983.

Curtis, Christopher Paul. *Bud, Not Buddy*. New York: Dell Publishing, 2002.

Dahl, Roald. *Charlie and the Chocolate Factory*. New York: Penguin Group, 2002.

——. *James and the Giant Peach*. New York: Penguin Group, 2000.

Defoe, Daniel. *Robinson Crusoe*. New York: Aladdin Books, 2001.

DiCamillo, Kate. *Because of Winn Dixie*. Cambridge, Massachusetts: Candlewick, 2000.

——. *Flora & Ulysses*. Cambridge, Massachusetts: Candlewick, 2013.

——. *The Tale of Despereaux*. Cambridge, Massachusetts: Candlewick, 2006.

Giff, Patricia Reilly. *Lily's Crossing*. New York: Random House, 1999.

Grahame, Kenneth. *The Wind in the Willows*. New York: Aladdin Books, 1989.

Hamilton, Virginia. *The House of Dies Drear*. New York: Aladdin Books, 2006.

Hesse, Karen. *Out of the Dust*. New York: Scholastic Press, 1997.

Kellogg, Stephen. *Johnny Appleseed*. HarperCollins, 1988.

Kinney, Jeff. *Diary of a Wimpy Kid,* The Long Haul. New York: Amulet Books, 2007.

Kipling, Rudyard. *The Jungle Book*. New York: Puffin Books, 2003.

Konigsburg, E. L. *The View from Saturday*. New York: Simon & Schuster, 1996.

London, Jack. *The Call of the Wild*. New York: Aladdin Books, 2003.

Lowry, Lois. *Anastasia Krupnik*. New York: Dell Publishing, 1979.

Montgomery, L.M. *Anne of Greene Gables*. New York: Aladdin Books, 2001.

Naylor, Phyllis Reynolds. *Shiloh*. New York: Dell Publishing, 1991.

Norton, Juster. *The Phantom Tollbooth*. New York, Random House, 2005.

O'Brien, Robert. *Mrs. Frisby and the Rats of NIMH*. New York: Aladdin Books, 1986.

Paterson, Katherine. *The Great Gilly Hopkins*. New York: HarperCollins, 1987.

——. *The Witch of Blackbird Pond*. New York: Random House, 1972.

Peck, Richard. *A Long Way from Chicago*. New York: Penguin Group, 2004.

——. *A Year Down Yonder*. New York: Penguin Group, 2002.

Riordan, Rick. *The Lightning Thief*. New York: Disney Hyperion, 2009.

Shakespeare, William. *Romeo and Juliet*. New York: Simon & Schuster, 2004.

Shelley, Mary. *Frankenstein*. New York: Simon & Schuster, 2004.

Speare, Elizabeth George. *The Witch of Blackbird Pond*. New York: Random House, 1978.

Spinelli, Jerry. *Maniac Magee*. New York: Little, Brown & Co., 1999.

Spyri, Johanna. *Heidi*. New York: Aladdin Classics, 2000.

Stevenson, Robert Louis. *A Child's Garden of Verses*. New York: Simon & Schuster, 1999.

——. *Treasure Island*. New York: Aladdin Books, 2000.

Twain, Mark. *The Adventures of Tom Sawyer*. New York: Aladdin Classics, 2001.

White, E. B. *Charlotte's Web*. New York: HarperCollins Publishers, 1952.

NOTES

Printed in Great Britain
by Amazon